POEMS AND READINGS
FROM MEDITATION

POEMS AND READINGS FROM MEDITATION

BRIAN PATTIMORE

APEX PUBLISHING LTD

First published in 2003 by

Apex Publishing Ltd

PO Box 7086, Clacton on Sea, Essex, CO15 5WN, England

www.apexpublishing.co.uk

British Library Cataloguing-in-Publication Data
A catalogue record for this book
is available from the British Library

ISBN 1-904444-09-1

Typeset in 11pt Times New Roman

Cover Design Jenny Parrett

Printed and bound in Great Britain

Introduction

I am a married man with four daughters, I always had a feeling that I could sometimes see and hear the spirit world but never really took much notice. It was about six months after Ruth my wife with a friend started to go to Bitterne Spiritualist Church the date was July 2000. I thought one Sunday I would go with them and see what it was all about. From the very first time that I walked through the church doors I felt really at ease with myself and thoroughly enjoyed the service. It was from that date that I started to go to church every Sunday and would feel disappointed if for some reason I could not make it to a Sunday service. I soon became interested in all the workshops that the church put on and attended every workshop possible. It was during these workshops that I learnt to meditate and within a short while I received my first poem titled By The Sea. It was to be quite awhile before my next poem was to come to me, and this was when my mother passed away in April 2001 the poem being Thank You, from then on the poems and readings were to come at a very fast rate, sometimes one a day. I feel that it is my Mother and Grandmother who are inspiring me to do this writing. I would like to dedicate this book to Ruth and everyone at Bitterne Spiritualist Church that has helped me on my spiritual pathway.

- Brian Pattimore

Thank You

Thank you Mum for giving me life
Thank you for sharing all my strife

Thank you, Mum for being there
Thank you, for all your loving care

Thank you, Mum for showing the way
When I was about to stray

Thank you, Mum for many things
Thank you, for all the joy you bring

Thank you, Mum with all my heart
I now know we had to part

But when I pass to over there
I know you'll be there
With all your loving care

Thank you
Love
Brian

- 1 May 2001

By The Sea

As I walk along the shore
I stop and looked at what I saw,
Ships that sail on by
Friends and family wave goodbye,
Children play on the sand
People walk hand in hand,
Oh how peaceful it can be
When you walk by the sea.

- 24 October 2000

I Will See You

I walk with you but I do not see you,
I talk to you but I do not hear you,
I feel your love through strands of light,
I now know that I am alright,
I feel your care and know that you are there

But come the day when I will see you
And come the day that I will hear you
Come the day that we can share all that loving care
For this will mean that I am there

We can walk hand in hand
All along the golden sand,
We can talk till our hearts content
Because there is no more pretence.

- 9 May 2001

Remember Me

Be not sad when I am gone,
But live your life full and strong
Think of me by your side
Think of me as the flowing tide,
I am but a thought away
I'll be with you everyday,
Shed no tears and have no fear
For I will always hold you dear.

When you walk through this land,
Let me be your guiding hand
And as you walk down life's long path
Think of all the things that's passed,
Some are good and some are bad,
But never let your heart feel sad.

Remember this each and everyday
I will hear all you say,
Let me know that you care,
For I will always hear your prayers
So think of me everyday
And I will help you on your way

- 12 May 2001

This World

This world was meant for all to see
So that we should all live in harmony.
This world was meant for fun and joy
Not for man to destroy.

Too many wars have come and past
How much longer can this last,
With famine all across this land
Let us lend a helping hand.

So many times we sit and pray
That mankind will find the way,
If man would only stop and see
We all should live in harmony

- 16 May 2001

My Guide

You know who I am for I am your guide, you know who I am
for I am by your side. You think of me and I am there, you
think of me and your troubles are shared. You know that I am
here for you, and I will help you think things through, so let
me help you understand, let me be your guiding hand. You
sometimes think you have seen me, you sometimes think you
have heard me, if only you would let things go you would
soon begin to know. So never think that I am not there, you
know we have time to share. So let me stay by your side, for I
am your life long guide.

- 23 May 2001

Think Things Through

You stayed right till the end
Now it's time to make amends
Please don't argue, fight, or row'
Please just let me rest for now

Remember all the times we had
And I will be forever glad
Just take a while to think things through
Then you will find what's best for you

I must leave for I must go
But please remember to take things slow
Think of me in things you do
You know I will come to you

- 25 May 2001

Stay Calm

When all around people scream and shout
Just stay calm and sort things out,
It doesn't matter if your right or wrong
Even if the day seems long
Just stay calm and sort things out.

People rush here and there
I often wonder if they really care,
Just stand back and take a hold
Many stories that are told
So just stay calm and sort things out.

Some people don't see eye to eye
Some even say goodbye,
Friendship is a special thing
Some just can't do the right thing.

If only they could stay calm
They soon would be walking arm in arm,
So just stay calm and sort things out
It takes awhile but it's all worthwhile
Just to see some people smile`
So take a rest and try your best
So just stay calm and sort things out

- 1 June 2001

If I Was Sure

As I walk down by the shore
Sometimes I feel that I am not sure,
When I walk on the sand
Did I really feel you touch my hand?

Did I hear that voice call me?
Or was it just a breeze in the trees,
If only I could see
All the spirits that walk with me.

Did I hear you say it's mum?
As I lay back in the sun,
Did I feel the summer breeze?
Or was it you come close to me.

Was that a thought?
Or was that a voice?
Now I have to make a choice.

Next time I feel you close to me
You'll fill my heart full of glee,
If only I could be sure
I will rest forever more.

- 21 June 2001

Don't Weep For Me

Don't stand and weep because I am gone,
Please go forward and grow strong.
I've learned life's secret with all it's wisdom,
Now I live in another kingdom.

Sit and listen and you'll hear,
All your loved ones drawing near,
So please don't weep because I am gone,
Just go forward and grow strong.

- 23 June 2001

Love

Love, what is love?
On one hand there is the kind of love that when you meet
someone and know that, from that moment you both want to
be together for the rest of your lives. Then there is family love
possibly one of the strongest kinds of love, but what if a
member of the family doesn't return your love? Well in my
view love is unconditional and that when you give love you
should not expect it back, that way if you give love and
receive nothing back you will not be disappointed.
Hopefully one day everyone will learn to give love and live
life peacefully. Do not harbour ill feelings for this will send
negative feelings to others around you, and they in turn will
find it hard to send love. Some people say they love life, but
what of those less fortunate than us do they hate their lives? I
think not. For the love that we send out to those less fortunate
than us will protect them and give them a sense that yes other
people do care and love them for who they are. After all they
are only following the path that has been set out for them and
at the end of it we will all meet and be equal.
So you see love is only a small word but has a big meaning to
our lives. So let all of us love our brothers, sisters, neighbours,
and yes even our enemies. For then and only then can the
meaning of love really start to take part in our lives and make
us a better person than we already are. So I send my love to
you in the hope you can find it in yourself to send it to others.

God Bless

- 1 July 2001

Memories

As I stroll down the lane
Memories come to me once again,
Look at the black bird building her nest
Soon her young will bring her no rest.

There's the field where I used to play
And watch the farmer harvest his hay,
How nice it used to be
Back in those days of '63.

But time moves on
And those days have gone,
Now I have young of my own
But how fast they seem to have grown
Soon they will leave me all alone.

But one things for sure
You will never hear me moan
For I will always have memories of my own.

- 1 July 2001

The Rose

Thank you for the rose you sent with your mother for me,
I will plant it in heavens garden and watch it grow
And one day I will bring it back to you ten fold
We walk with you everyday and yes,
We hear your loving prayers
When you feel that gentle breeze
You know its us trying to put you at ease.

- 4 July 2001

Spring

When spring time comes
The birds will sing,
While they are busy
Doing many things.

Baby rabbits
Hop here and there,
While their mother
Keeps aware.

For the first sign of danger
They must run
To their burrow under the ground.

Blue bells push through the hardened ground
Where ever you look
They're all around.

See them sway amongst the trees
In the springs gentle breeze

With each day that dawns
Another wonder is born
For life's mother nature
Never gets tired or worn.

So let's take a look
At natures show
And go in the knowledge
That you can grow

- 7 July 2001

14

My Dream Or Was It

After meditating I fell into a deep sleep where I had the most
wonderful dream. I dreamt that I went to the seaside for the
day where I decided to have my photo taken by a professional.
One hour later I went back to the shop to collect my photo. On
taking it out of the envelope to take a look you can imagine
my surprise when in the background there was my father. Now
as my father passed over eight years ago I asked the
shopkeeper how he had got my father in the picture. He told
me the gentleman had come in the shop with me and then
stood behind me while the photo was taken. On waking up I
realised it must have been a dream, how nice it would have
been to have that photo at least I have memories of that dream
"or was it"

- 18 July 2001

God Is there

God gave us life to enjoy
Doesn't matter if you're a girl or boy'
God gave us nature to explore
If you look very hard
You'll see even more.

God gave us four seasons
Starting with spring
God gave us the birds that sing

God made us all of one kind
So why can't man start to be kind,
We're all the same no matter what creed
So why do we have to have all this greed.

It takes a few seconds to say thank you or please
So why are some people so hard to please,
Hold out your hand and they might understand
That God is willing to lend a hand.

Look all around
And you will see
Many people that are in need,
Please take some time
And talk for awhile
You will make their lives more worthwhile.

So if you're sad and feeling low
Just take God's hand and you will glow,
This is God's way of letting you know
That he is there to help you grow

- 19 July 2001

Going Home

Don't be afraid for you won't be alone
Don't be afraid for you're going home,
Back to a place you left long ago
To live on the earth plain where you learnt to grow.

Don't be afraid for you won't be alone
Don't be afraid for you're going home,
Back to a place where the spirit's pain free
Where you can walk amongst the beautiful trees.

Don't be afraid for you won't be alone
Don't be afraid for you're going home,
Back to a place with bright sunlight
Back where the days never have nights.

Don't be afraid for you won't be alone
Don't be afraid for you're going home,
Back to a place where your loved ones your meet
Back to a place where old friends you will greet.

Don't be afraid if your body grows weak
Don't be afraid if you're to ill to speak,
For the time has come for you to go home
Back to Gods kingdom where you're not alone
Back to a place we all call home.

- 25 July 2001

I Come To You

I come to you time and again
I come to you to ease your pain,
Don't let your heart be sad
Lift up your spirit and be glad.

I am the warmth that flows through you
I am the one that's close to you,
Look at the stars on a moon lit night
For I am the star that shines so bright.

Listen to what I try to say
I am here to stay,
Think of a flower with its beauty so bright
I would love to hold you tight.

When you see the bright daylight
Never be afraid of the dark at night,
When you smell that sweet scent
You know that for you it is sent.

Don't sigh or moan
Think of me and you're never alone.

- 11 August 2001

Darkest Days

Your loves shines through on the darkest days
Spreading rays of light and warmth on its way,
Helping those in need
Always willing to do the good deed.

Spread your love across the land
Hold out your helping hand,
Never shy to show the way
To those who may want to stray.

From dark winter nights
To bright summer days
Your love will always light the way.
Let me show you all the days to come
Remember you too must have some fun,
Please slow down and take your time
You know your time is not all mine.

- 27 August 2001

There Is No Death

There is no death
For the spirit can not die,
There is no death just a short goodbye.

For we will meet once again
When its time to rid this body of pain,
Your loved ones will meet you
And guide you on your way.

To a place where all your fears are but a haze
Don't think of death as a final score
For really you're only going next door.

There is no death
For the spirit can not die,
Remember it's just a short goodbye.

- 29 August 2001

A Mother's Love

A mother's love is always there
A mother's love shows she cares,
When we are together we talk and laugh
How I wish this could last.

But one day I'll lose my glow
Then it will be time for me to go,
But don't despair
Think of the times we shared
For a mother's love is always there.

Spirit gave me this poem for my dear sister Marion

God Bless

- 2 September 2001

The Miner

Down in the valley where it is dark and grey
The look of dismay where the kids have to play,
Down on the coal face where it's dusty and dark
How the men long to see a sky lark.

They climb up the mountings where the air is pure and clean
At last they feel they can breath
Look down on the valley with its layer of smoke,
That's where we live and it's no joke.

Times are hard when you're digging for coal
When we soak and scrub
Still we can't move the colour of coal,
It's a sign of a miner with it deep in their skin.

But miners are hard and they take it on the chin
Chewing dust each and everyday is slowly eating my lungs
away.
There will come a time when we can't work any more
For the dust has done its worst
We find it hard to breathe with my life cut short.

And what was it for
Just to keep the home fires burning,
For a life of a miner is no fun
So take my advice and turn and run.
Stay above ground where man's meant to be
And enjoy the feeling of being free.

- 11 September 2001

Winter

Wintertime has come again
All it does is seem to rain,
Damp misty mornings
Dark gloomy nights,

How we thank God for giving us light.
Trees are bare with the leaves on the ground,
How we long for spring to come round
With new flowers breaking the ground.

Next will come summer
With long country walks,
Look at the sunset many colours so bright
Soon it will turn into night.

Then comes the autumn
Where the leaves turn gold, now the nights begin to get cold
The frost-laden mornings are now here
Sure sign that winter is near.

- 12 September 2001

Life's Ups And Downs

Life is full of ups and downs
Sometimes you feel you're given the run around,

You never get what your hearts desires
You always feel that you are tired,

Good things will come to those who wait
Good things will come when you show no hate,

For all God wants
Is for you to be kind,
And live in happiness
With mankind.

- 15 September 2001

The Dark Red Rose

A dark red rose will bloom in early June
Where two anniversaries are close to you,

At the moment your life feels low
And you are wondering which way to go.

Just follow the path that you have chosen
And you will learn all you want to know,

With help from a loved one
You hold very dear
Just like the rose it will bring us near.

- 25 September 2001

A Ring

A ring is a symbol of love,
So take this ring with my love
I am only a thought away,
No one can take our memories away
I love to cherish all you do
And go with the thought I am close to you,

- 27 September 2001

You And I

The oceans are wide
As wide as the sky,
Where lies a journey
For you and I

Creatures swim in the sea
Lots of colours for us to see,
There's a lot to explore as we learn even more
So look very hard and you'll see the shore.

An eagle flies high in the sky
One day who knows it will be you and I .

Life can be full of glory
And you are part of my life-long story.

For without you I cannot survive
You are the one that keeps me alive,
From the time your life begun
You and I are of one,

So trust in me and let's be free
For you and I have lots to see.

- 28 September 2001

Life's sting

You lay flowers when you come to me
You sit and talk for awhile when you come to me,

God bless, for it shows you care
May God walk with you everywhere,

For to walk in God's kingdom is a wondrous thing
For it takes away some of life's bitter sting,

Please keep on coming and having your chats
For you and I know there is no turning back,

The way is forward and to grow strong
And try to teach others to do no wrong.

- 5 October 2001

A Silent Prayer

I stand-alone by your grave
And say a silent prayer,
I stand alone and wonder why
You're not really there.

You now have gone to the spirit world
Where live life pain free,
You now live in the spirit world
Where you keep an eye on me.

I know that you are close to me
And hear my many thoughts,
I know that you are close to me
And in time will sort those thoughts.

I know that since you've been gone
I have to be strong,
And remember all the time you spent
Teaching me right from wrong.

Your love will never leave me
As mine will stay with you,
And I am sure between the two of us
We will see life's troubles through.

- 17 October 2001

Valley So Green

As I walk through this valley so green, I stop and remember
some of the things I've seen, Tulips and daffodils sway in the
sun, Children play in the park all having fun. I remember
talking to Mum and Dad and know they were there when I felt
so sad, to see a sunrise as it breaks a dark night, soon it will
shine so bright. With each new day is a wondrous thing and
during that day you'll learn many things. Some will be right
and some will be wrong. But never let your day seem long. So
when I am in this valley so green I know there's a lot I yet
haven't seen.

- 19 October 2001

September Day

Your world has yet another war
With hatred all around,

Bombs rain down from the sky
Making craters in the ground,

You say it's all for justice and someone has to pay,
For all those people that lost their lives
On that bright September day.

But killing's not the answer it goes against God's law
So send a little prayer that you'll
Have peace forever more.

- 27 October 2001

Time Gone By

The sun shines high in the sky
Shining down on you and I,
Many things we have to do
All made easier because I am with you.

Long summer days for us to spend
Talking to new and old friends.
When we stop and wonder why
So much time has passed us by.

There's so much we have to say
While we watch the children play.
When we sit and troubles we share
Then I remember how much you care.

Doesn't matter when I am feeling down
I soon become happy because you're around.
Now the time for you and I
To catch up on the time gone by.

- 5 November 2001

I Lay And Dream

As I lay and dream at night
I know that I won't feel the fright,
For God is my protector
And he'll guide me through the night,
And when I wake to bright sunlight
I'll know that I was right.

My loved ones came to see me
And reminisced old times,
And all the things they told me
I'll remember for a life time.

So when my life is over
And I've learnt all there is to know,
I'll go and meet my loved ones
That I dreamt of long ago.

- 7 November 2001

My Favourite Place

The sea breeze blowing on my face
As I sit in my favourite place,
Watching the world go by
I think of my life that's gone by,
All the memories bring a smile to my face
As I sit in my favourite place.

Life's too short and we're not here long
Time to put right all those wrongs,
Soon I'll hear the angels song
Where have all those times gone,
I guess this is how my life ends
Time now to meet my spirit friends.

Now my spirit has been set free
I'll go and sit in that cool sea breeze,
So as I sit in my favourite place
I know my life's over in the world's rat race,
All spirit people take things slow
And I can come back and let you know
How much I love you and miss you so.

- 19 November 2001

Life's A Candle

Life is like a candle
Glowing with all it's might

Life is like a candle
That lights the darkest night,

Life is like a candle
Blowing in the wind,

Life is like a candle
It's light will never dim,

Life is like a candle
It burns for you and I,

Life is like a candle
That we share until we die,

- 29 November 2001

Your Love

Your love will never leave me
As mine will stay with you,
And I am sure between the two of us
We'll see life's trouble through.

- 22 November 2001

Christmas Time

Christmas is a time of cheer, time to have your family near,
But spare a thought for those who passed,
And know that their love will last.

Christmas is a time of joy
Watching the children play with their toys,
Faces of sheer delight
Of all the presents Santa brought last night.

Christmas is a time of peace, time for all the fighting to cease,
Surely man can unite if only for one night
And make a pledge to give up the fight.

Christmas is a time of love, giving, and sending,
Your love is never ending.

Christmas is a time for being kind
Thinking of others that go without,
Trying your best to help them out
So all it takes for the world to unite,
Is to send out a thought on Christmas night.

- 23 November 2001

Christmas Has Come Around

Christmas has come around
With snow laying all over the ground,
Many places for Santa to go
As he travels through the snow,
Bringing love and joy
To every little girl and boy.
Around the world in just one night
As the children all sleep tight.
Many presents he will bring
As his sleigh bells ring,
Down the chimneys they say he goes
With every house he leaves a loving glow.
Christmas has come around
With Santa doing his yearly round.

- 28 November 2001

Brothers

Brothers should be the best of friends, showing each other that rifts can mend. Brothers should try and get along, for we're not here on earth very long. A brothers love can mean many things, and we should remember the joy that it brings. We should all have our own opinions, but it never hurts to stop and listen. Some things we say out of anger and sorrow, only to find we will regret it tomorrow, if only we could admit we're wrong, I know for sure we could get along. We don't have to continue this fight,
Now the time to put things right.

- 9 December 2001

Everyday

For everyday I see the sunrise, I think of thee,
For everyday I see the flowers grow I think of thee,
For all the things I learn in life I know you're with me,
Life's a path that we choose to take
So that we may learn from our mistakes,
All these things could not have been
If you were not the spirit in me.

- 9 December 2001

If I Should Die

If I should die before I am old be not sad for I would have learnt all of my lessons on the earth plain, and am now able to return home with all the knowledge I have gained. If I should die before I am old remember the times we shared and that my life was all the better for the love we shared. Even though I am not here in the physical body I am here in the spirit body. I will try and comfort you and guide you for I am only a thought away. So if I die before I am old be not sad but be full of cheer for I will always be very near. By day I will walk by your side and at night I will be your guide so sleep now my dear and remember I am near.

- 13 December 2001

Religion

Religion takes on many forms and shapes, Hindu, Buddhism, Catholic, Church of England, Spiritualism, to name a few. But if you were to stop and take a good look at yourself and those around you, you will notice that we are all spirit, right from day one. It's just we choose our religion so as to learn about God, just listen to others how they describe their beliefs. Each and everyone of us uses the word God. Why is this you might ask yourself, well the answer is right in front of you. There is only one God. Just think how one divine spirit can send out so much love to so many people no matter what colour, or creed, or believes his love is unconditional to each and every one of us. Yet what do we do, we have wars, kill animals sometimes to extinction, all the things that were put on this earth for us to enjoy we always find a reason to either hunt, kill or destroy it. As we are all spirit first and for most. Why can't we start to love our neighbours? Take care of others in the third world countries? Give some thought to those as soon as they are able to walk are thought how to use a gun. Or shout abuse at others, is it no wonder that we have so much killing in this world. Our God as their God is one of the same, yes we are all going to see one day that there is only one God. And that when we meet him on our homeward journey we will then start to live in harmony, for the spirit world there is no fighting or wars or killing of animals. There is only love and the need to help others. The very same people that while we were on earth tried to kill or hate us. For we would have seen by now that we are all spirit, one and the same.

- 13 December 2001

You Came To Me

You came to me full of grace
With a radiant smile on your face,
You stood there in a bright beam of light
Even though it was the dead of night.
As we enter a new year I heard you whisper in my ear
Don't be sad for I am here I will share in all your cheer,
Just raise a glass and remember me
And all my love you will see.

- 31 December 2001

An Angel

An angel comes so full of grace
Helping to put a smile on your face,
A guide is with you all your life
Sharing all your troubles and strife.
God is always willing for you to learn,
Life's too short to fall out with friends
For everyday that passes my life nears its end,
But I fear not I will not be scared
For I know my God will welcome me there.

- 5 January 2002

Your Day Through

When you feel that gentle breeze, when you feel the soothing stroke know it's me come close to you, helping you to see your day through. Don't dismiss that shadow you saw floating past an open door, feel at ease with that sweet smell of scent and know that it is heaven sent. Did you notice things have been moved especially when you're in a bad mood, know it's me come close to you helping you to see your day through. I am with you even though I've passed, for my love for you will always last. All those thoughts that come to you, helping you to see your day through. So when life's little things go wrong and the day seems more than twenty-four hours long. Know that I will come to you helping you to see your day through.

- 14 January 2002

Heaven's Door

Driving through fog so dense have some people got no sense, taking risks and what for, soon they could be knocking on heaven's door. And when they look back they will see, the speed they were doing was not necessary. For they would have got there all in good time, if only they had taken some more time. But now its too late risks they'll take no more, for now they are knocking on heaven's door.

- 15 January 2002

Harvest Time

As I watch the children play
I think of the farmer harvesting the hay.
For harvest time has come around
With the glow of a bright golden sun.

So let's help the elderly have some fun
They ask no thanks for what they've done.
They are the ones that taught us to walk and run.

So each harvest day that comes around
Remember the elderly for they to need some fun.

- 18 January 2002

When You Where Young

Remember when you were young
We would go for a walk in the sun
Down to the park where you could play
In the fields you would climb the bales of hay.
Now those days are in the past
Thank you God for the memories last,
Just think of those days with some pride
And know that I am by your side.

- 23 January 2002

Digging For Coal

Digging for coal to pay the bills, never having much time to be
ill, working in a space so cramped always
feeling the cold and damp.
The pit siren wails and all is not well for it means some poor
miner is trapped In this hell.
But for the lucky ones they can go home from working one
mile below. Out come the injured all battered and torn some
won't see the next day dawn.

And when they have cleared the rubble and mess back we go
to that cold pit face. Never knowing if this will be their last
shift feeling scared when the rafters shift, no please God not
again. Please let me see this day end.

- 30 January 2002

Down By The Trees

As you walk through the trees
There's so many things for you to see,
Look at the squirrels building their dray. Watch the flowers as
they break new ground the moles are busy building their
mounds. Soon it will be warmer and frogs start to spawn in a
few weeks tadpoles will be born.
Think of the sheep with their new born lambs spring is
now surely around.
When the dawn breaks and the cockerel crows
Its time once more to the woods we go.
Where each new day you will see life's mothe
nature living at ease.
With life's loving hand soon we will all understand God gave
us nature to admire and see.
Every time you walk down by the trees.

- 2 February 2002

Heaven's Not In The Sky

Heaven's not in the sky
It's here on earth right by your side,
Where your loved ones walk with you
where your guides can talk to you.

Heaven's a place we all adore
We quite often call it going next door,
And when we have done what we were sent here for
Then we can open that heaven's door.

Heaven's a place of love and peace
Where fighting and hating must cease,
For love is the true spirit law
And we all will know this
When we go next door

- 3 February 2002